PRA[illegible] EDUCATION

A RICH RESOURCE FOR TEACHERS, EDUCATIONALISTS AND CLERGY

Rupert Bristow

kevin mayhew

- *For the Revd Ben Tettey, who does his best to keep me spiritually aware.*
- *For my wife, Sarah, who does her best to keep me practically aware.*

kevin mayhew

First published in Great Britain in 2005 by Kevin Mayhew Ltd
Buxhall, Stowmarket, Suffolk IP14 3BW
Tel: +44 (0) 1449 737978 Fax: +44 (0) 1449 737834
E-mail: info@kevinmayhewltd.com

www.kevinmayhew.com

This edition published 2008

9 8 7 6 5 4 3 2 1 0

ISBN 978 1 84417 935 0
Catalogue No. 1501072

Cover design by Rob Mortonson
Typesetting by Fiona Connell Finch

Printed and bound in Great Britain

CONTENTS

FOREWORD

Teachers, educationalists and clergy will have collected stacks of resource material for prayer with children and young people. They will have rather fewer books of prayers about education. If they are at all like me, they will have remarkably few books of prayers for education, and even fewer that are in regular use.

I believe that Rupert Bristow has provided a collection of prayers that will be a rich resource for all those concerned with education in both its broadest and narrowest senses.

His long experience as a Christian teacher, educational administrator and Reader have combined to produce a collection that resonates powerfully with the life and concerns of people working in or connected with this field of human and godly endeavour. (It is also the fruit of some well-deserved study leave.)

I hope that the God who calls us to be his disciples will richly bless those who use these prayers, and those for whom they pray.

STEPHEN VENNER

Bishop of Dover and Bishop in Canterbury
Vice-Chairman, Board of Education of the Church of England

INTRODUCTION

Prayers are said daily in schools and other educational institutions throughout the country. There is no shortage of sources, old and new, for such prayers; and of course many of the best prayers come from the imagination and the moment.

In *Prayers for Education* my aim has been to provide prayers for particular purposes, which can be used as they are written or as templates for variations specific to the place or the event or the person. My hope is that wherever education takes place or its value is recognised, there will be a prayer here which can assist both laity and clergy, children and adults, in giving thanks or seeking God's guidance and help.

Under each heading there are usually two or more prayers, which should be regarded as alternatives. Italics denote wording that can be changed to suit individual preference and circumstances.

I also include some more personal, quick 'arrow' prayers which may meet a need in the midst of the chaos that education can sometimes be. And I make no apologies for including the prayer for all occasions and all situations, The Lord's Prayer, in both main versions.

In response to comments and suggestions, this second edition includes additional prayers under new subjects and headings. I am very grateful for the ideas, though I take full responsibility for the wording.

Rupert Bristow

1

BEGINNINGS

NEW SCHOOL YEAR

Almighty God

As we begin this new school year, we ask for your blessing on all who study and work here. May those who are new be helped by those who are returning.

May we accept new challenges with eagerness, new risks with courage, and new insights with openness.

Above all, Lord, assist us, in all our learning, to do our best and to grow in understanding of your world.

We ask this *through Jesus Christ, our Lord*

Amen

• • •

Almighty God

At the start of another year we come together to commit ourselves to our school community; to our learning and playing; and to each other.

Help us to bring forward all we have learnt last year to make the most of our time in this year's class.

Give us the strength and purpose, Lord, to be a good neighbour and a good Samaritan when others around us need our help.

We ask this *through Jesus Christ, our Lord*

Amen

NEW SCHOOL TERM

Heavenly Father

As a new term begins, we promise, with your help, to bring new energy to our work at this school.

May we always be aware of the needs of others in school and in the local community, including our church.

Help us to listen and learn in our classes; do our very best in our homework; and play our full part in school and class sports.

We ask this *in Jesus' name*

Amen

• • •

Heavenly Father

Thank you for the refreshment that the holidays have brought, for the people we have met and the places we have been.

As we gather again at the start of a new term, give us the energy to do our best, the desire to aim high and the ability to learn from our mistakes.

We pray for our teachers and our parents and ask that you care for them as they care for us.

We ask this *in Jesus' name*

Amen

NEW HEADTEACHER

Almighty God

We ask your blessing on our new headteacher . . . . . .

Give *him* wisdom and strength in the leadership *he* exercises.

May the school, the church and the wider community assist *him* in this role through personal, practical and prayer support.

And may *his* vision be your vision, Lord, as the school begins a new chapter in its history.

We ask this *through Jesus Christ, our Lord*

Amen

● ● ●

Almighty God

We give thanks for the arrival of our new headteacher . . . . . .

May *she* feel welcome and at home here at . . . . . . school.

Help *her* to meet your high expectations, Lord, and help us to show confidence in *her* leadership, renewing our commitment to the school's mission, and encouraging *her* through our support and prayer.

We ask this *through Jesus Christ, our Lord*

Amen

NEW PRIEST

Heavenly Father

As our new *priest* starts *his* ministry in this school and this community, we thank you for the gifts and experience *he* brings.

We look forward to *his* presence among us.

Help us to be responsive to *his* efforts to bring us closer to you and to your church, O God.

May *he* feel welcome and at home in our school and may our church be a place of worship, exploration and celebration for pupils, parents, staff and governors.

We ask this *in Jesus' name*

Amen

• • •

Heavenly Father

We celebrate the arrival of . . . . . . in our school community and in our church.

Give *her* energy, insight and patience in *her* ministry.

May our school play a full part in the church's life and worship and may our new *priest* always find a warm welcome in the school.

Through *her* words and work help us to know you better, to worship you joyfully and to give thanks for the love you have shown through your Son, Jesus Christ.

We ask this *in Jesus' name*

Amen

NEW BOARD OF EDUCATION

Almighty God

As our new Board gathers we ask for your strength and purpose to be clearly apparent in our deliberations.
Help each one of us to seek your will as we give direction to our work and the tasks ahead.

Keep us focused and alert; keep us open to the Holy Spirit.

Create in us a willingness to learn from each other, that we may grow your kingdom through our awareness of the needs of the children and families in our diocese, our educational communities, and our world.

We ask this *through Jesus Christ, our Lord*

Amen

• • •

Almighty God

We know that every child matters in your sight.

Help us as a new Board to see where we can bring the light of your love to shine on children, families and the work of education in our diocese.

Direct our thoughts, open our minds and empower us to take risks for your sake.

We ask this *through Jesus Christ, our Lord*

Amen

NEW STAFF

Heavenly Father

We celebrate the arrival of our new staff member(s) . . . . . . and ask your blessing on their contribution to our school.

May they bring new insights and gifts to our school life and may we welcome and support them in this new step in their career.

We ask this *in Jesus' name*

Amen

• • •

Heavenly Father

We ask for your guiding hand to be extended to our new staff member(s) . . . . . .

Let them flourish here as they become part of our team.

Give them firmness of purpose, generosity of spirit and willingness to listen. Give us the commitment to show hospitality, provide support and offer a Christian welcome.

We ask this *in Jesus' name*

Amen

NEW SCHOOL

Almighty God

We give thanks for our new school; for all those who planned, designed and built it; and for the vision that sustained the project.

May the learning and the teaching within these walls reflect that vision and your glory. And let us not take for granted our new surroundings, but appreciate them and allow them to enrich this learning community.

Wow . . .

We ask this *through Jesus Christ, our Lord*

Amen

• • •

Almighty God

Bring to these new buildings a sense of your presence.

Bring to our hearts a new purpose.

Bring to our learning and teaching a renewed commitment.

We give thanks for the dedication and expertise of all those who have contributed to this project and we ask for your blessing on those who will benefit from this school, now and in the years to come.

We ask this *through Jesus Christ, our Lord*

Amen

SCHOOL AMALGAMATION

Heavenly Father

As our two schools come together, please bless our new creation.

May we become stronger as we grow larger.

May we care for each other and share what both our schools have.

Above all, Lord, may we know you better through our worship together.

We ask this *in Jesus' name*

Amen

• • •

Heavenly Father

As we now become . . . . . . (school), help us to respect our different origins.

May we learn to think of ourselves as one community; our teachers, teaching assistants and support team as one staff; and our school aims as one shared vision.

Bring unity and purpose to our work and learning.

We ask this *in Jesus' name*

Amen

Almighty God

Create in us the will to work together and give us the means to collaborate effectively; enable the gifts of both our schools to flourish in our wider school community.

May your name be honoured and your Son's example followed in all that we do individually and together.

We ask this *through Jesus Christ, our Lord*

Amen

• • •

Almighty God

Bring to us new insights and new ways of working together.

May our schools bring to each other new opportunities for learning and growing forward together.

We ask that the collaboration we seek provides the challenge and change you ask of us all, through your transforming love.

We ask this *through Jesus Christ, our Lord*

Amen

NEW BUILDING

Heavenly Father

May this new building be an extension of your kingdom, a passport to new learning opportunities and a focus for excellence.

Help us to integrate what it can offer into the fabric of the school.

Inspire all those who use it with your purpose for them.

In sharing these facilities may the school and the community grow ever closer.

We ask this *in Jesus' name*

Amen

• • •

Heavenly Father

With this new building to inspire us, set our sights high.

With you as our guide, help us to enrich the education that goes on in this place.

May many people benefit from the new facilities and may skills learnt here reflect the skills which went into the building's design and construction.

We ask this *in Jesus' name*

Amen

NEW DAY

Almighty God

As our school day begins, we meet to dedicate ourselves to you.

May our hopes for today reflect your hopes for us.

Help us to face the challenges and take the opportunities that this day brings.

And in a moment of silence let us prepare ourselves for the tasks ahead . . . .

Be with us, Lord, in all that we do and say, and give us the time for reflection on our learning.

We ask this *through Jesus Christ, our Lord*

Amen

• • •

Almighty God

May this new day bring light as well as heat; help to overcome the hurdles; fun alongside the struggles.

Help us to put things in perspective, not to rush to judgement, and to listen hard to what others are saying.

May this school be a real learning community today.

We ask this *through Jesus Christ, our Lord*

Amen

2

ENDINGS

Almighty God

We give thanks for all that has been achieved in our school this year.

We remember our successes in competitions, as members of teams and as individuals. We recall the special occasions during the year when we went on visits, took part in a school production, involved visitors and contributed to a fun project.

Let us not forget the new things we have learnt during the year and the friendships we have made.

Prepare us, Lord, for all that the next school year will bring by granting us and our teachers and everyone in our school a great holiday.

We ask this *through Jesus Christ, our Lord*

Amen

• • •

Almighty God

May we look back on the year with pride at the things achieved, awareness of where we have gone wrong, and thanks for all that our teachers and parents have done for us.

We look forward to the holidays, remembering the friends we have made and all the new things we have learnt and experienced.

Bring us back refreshed and ready for all the next year will offer.

We ask this *through Jesus Christ, our Lord*

Amen

SCHOOL TERM

Heavenly Father

We are ready for the holidays. You know, Lord, that we have done our best and learnt a lot. Thank you for the fun we have had and the hard work we have put into this term. Help us to carry on learning after this short break.

We ask this *in Jesus' name*

Amen

• • •

Heavenly Father

As we complete another term, we give thanks for this school community, our class, our friends, our teachers, our teaching assistants, our parents and all who support the school.

Bring us back safely next term.

Just as we look forward to the holidays, so may we look forward to returning here to . . . . . . (school).

We ask this *in Jesus' name*

Amen

SCHOOL CLOSURE

Almighty God

We give thanks for . . . . . . (school):
for the vision of those who founded it;
for the headteachers and governors who have had charge of it;
for the Church which has supported it;
and for all the children who have been educated here.

We ask that all those who have learned and taught and administered in our school, and the parents who entrusted their children to the school's care will know your lasting love through their time here and will always have . . . . . . (school) in their hearts and minds.

We ask this *through Jesus Christ, our Lord*
Amen

• • •

Almighty God

In the ending of this chapter in our community's history, we give thanks for the education . . . . . . (school) has provided for the pupils here.

May all who have learned, taught and worked here be proud of those gifts they have shared and received.

Wherever people move on to, let a little part of . . . . . . (school) be carried with them to help them on their way.

We ask this *through Jesus Christ, our Lord*
Amen

RETIRING TEACHER/HEADTEACHER

Heavenly Father

As we say goodbye to . . . . . . we thank you for *his* tireless work for this school.

We remember the special ways in which *he* has made *his* mark on our school and our community – and how *he* has been special to each one of us.

Only you, Lord, know how hard *he* has worked on our behalf.

Bring *him* a long, happy and fulfilling retirement in the knowledge that *he* has carried out your purpose here.

We ask this *in Jesus' name*

Amen

• • •

Heavenly Father

We celebrate all that . . . . . . has meant to us here at . . . . . . (school): in the classroom, in the hall, in *her* office, on the playing field, and also in the community.

Thank you, Lord, for the special gifts *she* has shared with pupils and staff over . . . . . . years at this school.

Bring *her* happiness and good health in retirement, fond memories of this place and a sure knowledge of firm friendships made and a job well done.

We ask this *in Jesus' name*

Amen

RETIRING (LEAVING) PRIEST

Almighty God

We thank you for the ministry of . . . . . . in our school.

As we say farewell to *him* we remember the many ways
in which *he* has supported the school, leading worship
at our assemblies, making us feel at home in the church,
and being available in good times and difficult times.

May . . . . . . continue to serve you, Lord, in your church,
knowing that *he* leaves us firmer in our faith
and with a closer relationship with you.

We ask this *through Jesus Christ, our Lord*

Amen

• • •

Almighty God

We are grateful that you sent . . . . . . to this school
and this community to be our pastor and our friend.

We celebrate *her* ministry amongst us as we say farewell
to *her* (and *her* family).

Through *her* we got to know you better, Lord.

May the link between the school and the church continue
to flourish, building on the firm foundations which you have
laid here through the ministry of . . . . . .

Bestow your blessings on *her* in the next stage of *her* work
in your service.

We ask this *through Jesus Christ, our Lord*

Amen

STAFF LEAVING

Heavenly Father

We give thanks for the contribution that . . . . . . has made to the life of this school.

As we say farewell, we remember all that *he* has meant to us previously, all that *he* has done for the school as a whole, and *his* contribution to the wider community.

As *he* moves on from this school, Lord, may *he* be aware of your love in all *his* future endeavours.

We ask this *in Jesus' name*

Amen

• • •

Heavenly Father

We will miss . . . . . . in our school.
We will miss all the things that make *them* special:
her sense of humour,
his . . . .

We will laugh when we remember
her big earrings,
his odd socks.

Please, Lord, look after *them* when *they* leave,
and may *they* have many good memories of us too.

We ask this *in Jesus' name*

Amen

GOVERNOR LEAVING

Almighty God

As . . . . . . steps down from being a governor here, we celebrate *his* commitment to this school during the past . . . . years.

You know, Lord, the late hours and many days *he* put in and you know the difference *he* has made.

In asking for your blessing on *him* we also ask for your continued inspiration in the work of governors in the years to come.

We ask this *through Jesus Christ, our Lord*

Amen

• • •

Almighty God

We will miss the contribution . . . . . . has made to our deliberations, our decisions and our debates.

We ask, Lord, that you will continue to use *her* ministry in other ways to extend your kingdom.

We thank you for *her* lasting legacy to our school and our community.

May *her* contribution be an indication of our desire to serve you always.

We ask this *through Jesus Christ, our Lord*

Amen

END OF DAY

Heavenly Father

We offer you our day's work.

As we prepare to go home, help us to reflect on what we have learnt, what we have seen, what we have said, what we have struggled with, and what we have enjoyed.

We are sorry for any angry words or unjust actions.

We thank you, Lord, for the whole day and look forward to what tomorrow will bring.

We ask this *in Jesus' name*

Amen

• • •

Heavenly Father

Thank you for our school day.

Thank you for revealing more of your world to us.

Thank you for all the experiences this day has brought.

May our school always be a learning community with you as its focus, Lord.

Give us rest tonight so that we can return refreshed and ready to resume our studies.

We ask this *in Jesus' name*

Amen

Almighty God

We ask for your blessing on all who are moving on to their next school.

We give thanks for what they have contributed to this school, what they have learnt and what they have left behind them.

May they be a credit to our school in all that they achieve in their future lives and may they remain grateful for what this school has given them.

We ask this *through Jesus Christ, our Lord*

Amen

• • •

Almighty God

We thank you for the achievements and hard work of all those who are leaving this term; for the friendships they have made; for the service they have given.

We ask, Lord, for your protection and inspiration as they move on to the next step in their education, the next development of your purpose for them.

May they remember the Christian values they have learnt in this school and may they always follow your ways.

We ask this *through Jesus Christ, our Lord*

Amen

3

CELEBRATIONS

EDUCATION SUNDAY

Usually, but not exclusively, celebrated on the ninth Sunday before Easter

Almighty God

As we celebrate all that education can offer us and all that we can bring to education, we give thanks for the role of the church in our schools and the contribution of schools to the life of our church.

Help those who teach and those who learn to build on these links.

Grant wisdom to governors of schools and to PCC members, to diocesan and council officers, and to national government in sustaining and developing the educational system in all its depth and breadth.

And in their growth of understanding and knowledge, may all pupils seek to love you, as you love them.

We ask this *through Jesus Christ, our Lord*

Amen

• • •

Almighty God

On this special Sunday we pray for the schools and colleges we serve.

May those who study prosper and grow in their learning.

Enable those who teach, support, administer or govern to carry out their duties with commitment and energy, knowing they have the support of this congregation through our prayers and in our actions.

Show us, Lord, new ways of expressing and developing the church's partnership with our schools and colleges.

We ask this *through Jesus Christ, our Lord*

Amen

SIGNIFICANT ANNIVERSARIES

Heavenly Father

As we celebrate the school's . . . . . . years of service to our community,
we give thanks for those who have learned about you here;
those who have grown in faith here and those
who have made . . . . . . a special place.

May the staff and governors, parents and pupils
always value their time and each other's efforts at
this school.

May they look back in appreciation and forward in hope.

Give to this learning community the confidence
to make a difference,
to challenge what is wrong
and champion what is right,
and to grow daily in our love for you.

We ask this *in Jesus' name*

Amen

• • •

Heavenly Father

On this special day for the school we give thanks for all those who have contributed to the life of this place. Thank you for the commitment of the people who founded the school and for all the teaching and learning that has taken place here.

We ask that your Church continues to provide us with support and prayer, inspiration and love.

We ask this *in Jesus' name*

Amen

Almighty God

It's a great day.

Please be with us as we celebrate and have fun.

Help us to value what we have and not worry about what we don't have.

Thank you for all those who have built up our school and the community around us, and we ask you to bless everyone in our school today.

We ask this *through Jesus Christ, our Lord*

Amen

• • •

Almighty God

It is only . . . . . . years since we became . . . . . . (school).

We have enjoyed the journey so far and we look ahead with confidence and expectation.

Be with us on our journey, in our church,
in our community, in our school and in our hearts.

We ask this *through Jesus Christ, our Lord*

Amen

NEW BIRTH

Heavenly Father

As we welcome back our (head)teacher we celebrate the arrival of their child. We thank you for the gift of a new life and ask that the family of this school be an extension of their own.

Bring happiness and a bright future to . . . . . .

We ask this *in Jesus' name*

Amen

• • •

Heavenly Father

As we celebrate the arrival of a new brother/sister for . . . . . . we pray for all new-born babies around the world.

In these early weeks of life, bring renewed efforts to all who care and protect the new-born.

May love combine with nursing and medical care to safeguard their health.

May adequate nourishment be available wherever it is needed and not just where it is wanted.

May hope overcome adversity.

We ask this *in Jesus' name*

Amen

Almighty God

As we receive and celebrate our school's inspection report(s), we acknowledge and give thanks for all the hard work represented and recognised in the report(s).

You know, Lord, the strengths of this school community.
You know our weaknesses too.

May we grow forward together in confidence and in faith so that we can continue to be worthy of your purpose.

We ask this *through Jesus Christ, our Lord*

Amen

• • •

Almighty God

Great news!

We pray that these reports are read and valued by staff, governors, parents and pupils and recognised as part of your 'good news' too, Lord.

Help all those in our community to see our school as we really are and to support us in all our activities.

May we continue to grow as a learning community.

And may your church be at the heart of our school life.

We ask this *through Jesus Christ, our Lord*

Amen

SPEECH/PRIZE DAY

Heavenly Father

Today we celebrate achievement.

But we know, Lord, that our efforts are in vain without you.

So we give thanks for all the opportunities that this school has provided, the dedication of the staff and the support of our parents.

As we applaud the excellence and service of the prize-winners we remember the progress we have all made and, in a moment of silence, we bring before you our own special memory of an achievement this year . . . . . .

May all we do be offered to you, Lord.

We ask this *in Jesus' name*

Amen

• • •

Heavenly Father

Every person is special in your sight.

We know that this school is also special to you, Lord.

Let today be a celebration of achievements for individuals and teams, but also a celebration of the life of this school and its place in our community.

We give thanks for the hard work of teachers, support staff and governors which has enabled us all to give our best, to learn from each other and to serve you.

In applauding the prize-winners may we also applaud you, Lord.

We ask this *in Jesus' name*

Amen

SPORTS DAY

Almighty God

You have given us strength and judgement as well as knowledge.

Be with us today as we use your gifts in our races and jumps and games.

Help us to use our individual skills and our teamwork to the maximum.

Above all, Lord, let us have fun on our sports day.

We ask this *through Jesus Christ, our Lord*

Amen

• • •

Almighty God

We ask for your blessing on our sports day.

We pray that in all our races, jumps and throws we try to exceed our personal best. Where we are part of a team, in relays and games, may we do our best to support others to succeed in the interests of the team.

And may we compete fairly, perform safely and not laugh too much when our parents take part.

We ask this *through Jesus Christ, our Lord*

Amen

DIFFERENT FAITHS

Almighty God

As we gather as people of faith, we thank you for
the different paths we have been given to follow;
the different ways in which we can worship you;
the different ways we have experienced your love.

In our lives and in our minds, may we remain true to you
and respectful of each other's different contributions;
may we always be aware of, and celebrate,
the rich diversity of your world.

Amen

• • •

Loving God

Bring to us an understanding of different cultures and different faiths.

Help us to recognise what binds us together as human beings, what divides us through background and history, and what we can do to understand each other better.

May we push back the limits of our learning,
knowing that there are no boundaries in your creation.

Amen

Lord God

In our learning about different religions,
help us to hold on to what we believe
and reach out to explore and celebrate what is new.

May we respect the views and beliefs of others.
Create in us, Lord, the capacity to understand and reflect.

Help us to learn fresh ways of being still and knowing that you are God.

Amen

• • •

Lord God

On this day when the festival of . . . . . . is celebrated, we thank you for the richness of cultures and religions in your world.

We pray especially for all those in our community and all those worldwide for whom this is a special day.

You gave us all the gift of hospitality. Let us offer and receive that gift as we celebrate and give thanks.

Amen

4

DISASTERS, SETBACKS, FAILURES AND FORGIVENESS

DISASTERS

Almighty God

Help us to understand what has happened, Lord.

Give strength to those who are still suffering – the homeless, the hungry, those who have lost loved ones, those who have lost the will to live.

Show your love to them, give them hope and show us the way to help.

We ask this *through Jesus Christ, our Lord*

Amen

• • •

Almighty God

We do not know why this disaster has struck . . . . . .
You know all those who have been hurt. You know all those who have been killed. You know all those who are still missing. We pray especially for anyone we know who has been affected; give us the insight to find the ways in which our school can be of assistance.

Meanwhile we pray for the rescue services and we hope for speedy recovery.

We ask this *through Jesus Christ, our Lord*

Amen

SETBACKS

Heavenly Father

We pray for our school community at this difficult time.

Help us to recover and rebuild our confidence.

Give strength to our teachers and governors as they meet the challenges ahead.

May pupils and parents join them in preparing
for a better future.

Make us proud in our school and in all the people
who contribute to our learning community.

We ask this *in Jesus' name*

Amen

• • •

Heavenly Father

Help us to come to terms with . . . . . . that has hit our school so hard.

Give us the help and the hope from all around to put us back on our feet.

We put our trust in you, Lord, to bring out the best in us at this time.

May our neighbours in this community act as good neighbours and may we repay them by redoubling our efforts in all that we do.

We ask this *in Jesus' name*

Amen

FAILURES AND FORGIVENESS

Almighty God

We admit our many failures before you, Lord,
and before each other.

You know the difference between failure without trying
and failure despite trying hard.

We know you are a forgiving God. Forgive our
shortcomings and help us to learn from the things
we do wrong or do badly.

We ask this *through Jesus Christ, our Lord*

Amen

• • •

Almighty God

Bring us to realise our faults and our failures, we pray.

In a moment of quiet let us think of one thing we have done
wrong and for which we are very sorry . . . . . .

Give us and our families and friends a new spirit of support,
love and forgiveness.

Help us not to be selfish and to respect others, however
difficult that sometimes seems.

We ask this *through Jesus Christ, our Lord*

Amen

5

GRACES

Almighty God

We give thanks for this food: for those who grew it;
for those who brought it here; for those who prepared it;
for those who cooked it; and for those who serve it.

Now we ask for your blessing on those who eat it.

Amen

• • •

Almighty God

As we sit down to eat our lunch, let us remember all that has gone into the preparation of this meal.

Help us to be aware also, Lord, of those in the world who are short of food and water, for whom our meal would be a feast.

Amen

• • •

Almighty God

You provide for our every need.

Help us to appreciate what is now before us.

Bless this food to our use and strengthen us in your service.

Amen

Heavenly Father

We are looking forward to our meal.

Let us do justice to this food, remembering that we cannot take it for granted.

Thank you for the skills of all those involved in providing our lunch today.

Amen

• • •

Heavenly Father

This food you give to us.

Our praise we give to you.

Amen

6

OCCASIONAL PRAYERS

AT A GOVERNORS' MEETING

Almighty God

May we bring reflection and wisdom to our meeting.

Use our expertise and our judgement, Lord, in directing our contributions.

Let us be listeners more than speakers.

And may we always have in mind your will
for the well-being and the future of the school.

We ask this *through Jesus Christ, our Lord*

Amen

• • •

Almighty God

We pray for our school and our meeting: grant us the wit and the wisdom to conduct our business in a good spirit, open to the views of others but firm in the purpose of our endeavour, and guided by your will.

May our decisions always support the mission of this school and your church.

We ask this *through Jesus Christ, our Lord*

Amen

AT A STAFF MEETING

Heavenly Father

Be with us as we meet.

Guide us as we talk.

Stay with us as we plan.

Open our ears as we listen.

Open our eyes to your vision.

We ask this *in Jesus' name*

Amen

• • •

Heavenly Father

In our meeting, help us to focus on what is important rather than just what is urgent.

May everything we discuss have a bearing on the children in our charge.

Let us never forget that it is both a privilege and a responsibility to play a part in the education of the young.

Grant that we always support each other in that process.

We ask this *in Jesus' name*

Amen

AT AN ANNUAL/OCCASIONAL MEETING WITH PARENTS

Almighty God

As we mark another year of effort and achievement at our school, we gather to hear the report of the governors and questions of parents.

We pray that in our report and in our questions we can reflect the mission of our school and your purpose for us.

Guide all those involved in the school in the paths of righteousness and the search for truth.

We ask this *through Jesus Christ, our Lord*

Amen

• • •

Almighty God

We pray for this school.

We give thanks for the staff and pupils.

We ask for your encouragement to governors and parents.

Help us to take stock of the past year, to acknowledge achievements and to be clear-sighted about improvements under way.

Bring insight to our meeting and understanding to our hearts.

We ask this *through Jesus Christ, our Lord*

Amen

AT EXAM TIME

Heavenly Father

We pray for all those taking exams today/this week.

You know their capability, Lord.

Help them to do themselves justice as they are put to the test.

Give them the confidence and strength to show what they have learnt, to demonstrate their ability to analyse, and to prove that they can express themselves.

Banish any nerves and give them the peace to show themselves as they really are.

We ask this *in Jesus' name*

Amen

• • •

Heavenly Father

Help and guide us as we sit our exams.

May we recall what we have learnt.

Keep our minds focused as we analyse and solve problems,
let our imagination soar as we express ourselves,
but help us to remember to do the simple things well.

May Jesus be our example and inspiration as we are put to the test.

We ask this *in Jesus' name*

Amen

AT CONFIRMATION

Almighty God

As the faith of . . . . . . is confirmed we ask that *he* is upheld and supported in *his* beliefs by all present today.

May this significant milestone in *his* faith journey
be a source of inspiration for *him* and a creative
opportunity for the church.

We pray that through your grace and *his* faith,
his life may be strengthened and your kingdom extended.

We ask this *through Jesus Christ, our Lord*

Amen

• • •

Almighty God

We pray for those being confirmed today.

May your high expectations, Lord, be matched by their faithfulness.

On this special occasion, when their baptism is transformed into confirmation by your grace and their free will, let this church rejoice and their school(s) applaud.

May the sacraments deepen their spiritual experience of you and encourage them in the exploration of their faith.

In a moment's silence let us pray for the individual(s) being confirmed . . . . . .

Let us pledge ourselves to doing all we can to support them in their commitment.

We ask this *through Jesus Christ, our Lord*

Amen

DEATH OF A PUPIL

Heavenly Father

We give thanks for the life of . . . . . .; for the smiles, the fun and the friendships *she* brought to our lives.

Through our tears we ask, Lord, that as *she* is welcomed into your loving arms *she* also stays in our hearts.

She will always be special to . . . . . . school and to . . . . . . church.

Help us all, family, friends and community, to say farewell to . . . . . . but never to forget *her*.

We ask this *in Jesus' name*

Amen

• • •

Heavenly Father

At present we can only feel the loss of . . . . . .

We want to be strong and we want to understand why *he* is no longer here with us.

We pray that . . . . . . is safe in your arms, in your heavenly kingdom.

Help us to remember what *he* meant to us and what *he* left behind – the laugh, the smile, the favourite comment, the things *he* struggled with.

Bring us happy memories in the tears.

Bring *him* the peace only you can give, Lord of love and mercy.

We ask this *in Jesus' name*

Amen

DEATH OF A TEACHER/HEADTEACHER

Almighty God

You know that it will be difficult for us at . . . . . . school without . . . . . .

Bring us the strength and the hope to carry on, as *he* would have wished.

We thank you, Lord, for the special gifts *he* brought to this school and shared with us.

May the church and the wider community give thanks for *his* contribution to the life of . . . . . . (village/town) and may we redouble our own efforts to serve each other, in honour of *his* memory.

We ask this *through Jesus Christ, our Lord*

Amen

• • •

Almighty God

As we remember all that . . . . . . has meant to us at . . . . . . school, we pray that *she* is now at peace with you in your eternal kingdom.

Only you know why *she* was taken from us at this time, but we give thanks for *her* special place in our hearts at our school.

We pray for *her* family and friends at this difficult time.

Show your love for them and for us as we struggle to cope with the loss.

May your church be a comfort and a strength to us all.

We ask this *through Jesus Christ, our Lord*

Amen

7

INTERCESSIONS AT SUNDAY SERVICES

Almighty God

Inspire those who exercise their vocation as teachers, lecturers, governors, support staff or helpers.

In our community we pray especially for . . . . . . and for the place(s) of education with which we have a personal link.

Grant wisdom to all who are responsible for education planning, teacher training and policy making.

We pray also for the work of our chaplains that their ministry may be sustained and upheld.

In our wider community we pray for our local authority and for the Diocesan Board of Education.

We ask this *through Jesus Christ, our Lord*

Amen

• • •

God of Hope, may your light guide our educational path.

God of Hunger, may we feed on your wisdom and thirst for your truth.

God of Healing, may you bring learning out of failure, humility from success.

God of Help, may we be a good Samaritan to others.

God of Habit, may we grow in faith and devotion.

We ask this *through Jesus Christ, our Lord*

Amen

Heavenly Father

We give thanks for the many opportunities for learning in our schools and community.

We pray for our junior church, for the uniformed organisations and for the mother and toddler group.

We ask for your blessings on those recently confirmed or planning to be confirmed.

We thank you that we have the responsibility and legacy of our church school, where excellence and faith can go hand in hand, Lord. Inspire us all to use our particular skills in the educational institutions in our community.

We ask this *in Jesus' name*

Amen

• • •

Heavenly Father

We pray for all pupils and students; we give thanks for the window on your creation that their education provides, for the horizons that are in their reach and for the foundations of wisdom.

Give them the power to reflect on the source of all knowledge.

Help our nurseries, schools, colleges and universities to provide a framework for lifelong learning.

We pray especially for headteachers and principals.

We ask this *in Jesus' name*

Amen

8

MEDITATION

A MEDITATION FOR TEACHERS AND LEARNERS

Our Lord and our God

You have created us in your image;
you have given us the freedom to know or deny you;
you see into our hearts and minds.
Set us on the right course to your still centre;
guard us and guide us when we do your will;
forgive us when we fall short of your plan for us.
Above all, God, hold us close, take away our fear.

Silence

Our God and Father

Teach us your ways, O God, so that we can know you better and make you better known;
teach us to search for you in those around us,
in our families, in our churches, in our places of learning,
in unexpected places and people.

Teach us to love and trust you,
as we are loved and trusted by you, Lord;
teach us to take on new challenges, sacrificial
responsibilities, and fresh expressions of faith
for each new generation.

Above all, Lord, teach us to learn, encourage us to sow good seeds, empower us to witness to your love and forgiveness.

Silence

Our Father and Lord

Bring wisdom and enthusiasm to our schools, colleges and universities and to all who teach, learn and plan; bring a pastoral sensitivity and inspirational vision to our leaders, ordained and lay, elected and appointed, national and local.

May your Church make a difference in proclaiming that every child matters to you.

May talk of transformation focus on people's lives and be based on values taught by your Son.

Above all, Lord, help us to take care and take risks to bring your kingdom closer to us and all those we serve.

Silence

The grace of our Lord Jesus Christ,
and the love of God,
and the fellowship of the Holy Spirit
be with us all evermore.
Amen

9

PRAYERS AT CHURCH MEETINGS

AT A SYNOD

Almighty God

May our synod today bring enlightenment to the educational issues being debated.

Help us to honour the gifts of learning and teaching as we discuss the process of education.

Let us be alert to opportunities for the church to bring wholeness and hope to our places of learning through the work of Christian teachers and governors, staff and pupils, priests and laity.

Give direction to our efforts, Lord, and purpose to our decisions, so that we can make a difference to education in our *diocese*.

We ask this *through Jesus Christ, our Lord*

Amen

• • •

Almighty God

As this synod debates the church's stake in education, help us to focus on the example of your Son as teacher: challenging, explaining and clarifying.

In our differing perspectives on the mechanics of education, let us hold fast to the importance of setting the spirit free in all our learning communities.

Help us to be creative and thoughtful as we seek to discern your will for our work.

We ask this *through Jesus Christ, our Lord*

Amen

AT A PCC MEETING

Heavenly Father

Inspire us with your wisdom.

School us in your knowledge.

Educate us in your ways.

May our discussions help to bring your kingdom nearer and make our purpose clearer.

Show us how education can help to reveal your glory.

We ask this *in Jesus' name*

Amen

• • •

Heavenly Father

As we discuss our relationship with the schools and colleges in our parish, we pray for all those involved in education.

Help us to consider ways in which we can assist in fulfilling your high expectations of schools and pupils, colleges and students.

May we be ever present, as your representatives, to celebrate success and to console in difficult times.

Strengthen our church in its mission to support the places of education in our community.

We ask this *in Jesus' name*

Amen

AT THE BOARD OF EDUCATION

Almighty God

We pray for the schools, colleges and universities
in this diocese.

In our deliberations today help us to seek ways
to strengthen your presence in all the institutions we discuss.

May our policies reflect your wisdom, our priorities be true
to your word and our decisions carry your authority.

Let us always be mindful of the legacy of our predecessors
and the long-term consequences of our actions.

We ask this *through Jesus Christ, our Lord*

Amen

• • •

Almighty God

We are guardians of your church's role in education,
especially in our church schools.

Help us to do all in our power, under your guidance,
to discuss the issues before us with the care, rigour
and thought we would expect in our places of learning;
let us not fall short of your high expectations in our policy
and decision-making.

We pray especially for schools and their churches facing
particular challenges at this time, and for the work of this
Board and its staff in giving appropriate support.

We ask this *through Jesus Christ, our Lord*

Amen

10

SCHOOL PRAYERS

PRIMARY SCHOOL

These prayers are meant to be models of what could be a school's own prayer, said regularly and on special occasions. However, they can also be used as 'one off' prayers in daily worship.

Almighty God

May our school be welcoming.

May our school be encouraging.

Let friendship flourish here.

Let learning fill our day.

Give us the strength to do our best.

Give us the hope to carry on.

Be our guide in all we do.

Lord, make this school your home too.

We ask this *through Jesus Christ, our Lord*

Amen

Almighty God

We give thanks for our school.

For us it is a special place.

Make it special for you, Lord, and bring your peace, love and friendship to everything we do here.

As we learn and as we play, may we always be in your safe keeping.

We ask this *through Jesus Christ, our Lord*

Amen

Heavenly Father

Be with us in our learning.

Be with us in our playing.

Be with us in our laughter.

Be with us in our tears.

Be with us when we get things right and when we get things wrong.

Be with us as we come to school and when we travel home.

We know that you will always be here for us, Lord, at . . . . . . school.

We ask this *in Jesus' name*

Amen

● ● ●

Heavenly Father

Help our learning and our knowing and bring us friendship and fellowship.

Take us to new places, Lord, as our teachers show us the wonders of your creation.

May we help each other at . . . . . . school so that we can learn from everyone around us.

We pray also for our families and our homes; keep them safe while we are safe at school.

We ask this *in Jesus' name*

Amen

SECONDARY SCHOOL

Almighty God

We pray for this school and all who contribute to its achievements as a place of learning.

Bring a sense of purpose to our work, a commitment to justice in our behaviour and a desire for integrity and wholeness in our being.

May we succeed with each other's help rather than at each other's expense.

May our ambitions for ourselves embrace your ambitions for us, Lord.

And may this school be a Christian presence in the wider community.

We ask this *through Jesus Christ, our Lord*

Amen

• • •

Almighty God

Help us to grow forward together in faith and fellowship.

Grant that both our worship and our work at this school reflect your purpose for us.

Help us to share our strengths and to learn from others as we try to overcome our weaknesses.

Bind us into a community, with you at the centre of our mission.

May this school be a beacon of hope and a source of inspiration under your guidance.

We ask this *through Jesus Christ, our Lord*

Amen

11

PRAYERS FOR CHURCH, COLLEGE AND UNIVERSITY

Almighty God

Guide your Church nationally to stay true to the vision that inspired the development of education in this country.

Help us to remember our responsibilities to those in our schools, colleges and universities and to rekindle the creative flame of our imagination in planning for future generations.

In reaffirming our faith in the future, be with us in the challenges ahead, prepare us for the celebrations and the setbacks, and above all, Lord, give us a glimpse of the breadth, length, height and depth of your love.

We ask this *through Jesus Christ our Lord*

Amen

• • •

Almighty God

We pray for the churches and schools across the world linked to us through the *Anglican Communion.*

We thank you for all those who have spread your word in lands far and near.

Make us open to learning about and learning from Christians in all parts of the world.

We especially pray for schools and colleges in . . . . .

We ask this *through Jesus Christ our Lord*

Amen

COLLEGE

Heavenly Father

May this college serve the surrounding community in ways which draw together the skills and needs of its people.

Give ambition to students, energy to lecturers and vision to managers of this institution.

May the culture of dedication among staff be reciprocated by a respect for learning among students.

We ask, Lord, that vocational pathways are found and are well travelled in this place.

We ask this *in Jesus' name*

Amen

Heavenly Father

We give thanks for the staff and students in this college,
the gifts they bring, the strengths they share
and the friendships they make.

Bring a spirit of openness and integrity to the teaching and learning that goes on here.

And may the wider community benefit from the skills, knowledge and judgement available at this college.

We ask this *in Jesus' name*

Amen

Almighty God

We ask for your blessings on . . . . . . college.

Bring us the wisdom to make the most of the learning experience, whether listening and observing, or sharing and doing.

May the focus of our education be excellence and service.

May the fruits of our work here promote lifelong learning in mind, body and spirit.

And may our college be a force for creativity, quality of life and care in our community.

We ask this *through Jesus Christ, our Lord*

Amen

UNIVERSITY

Heavenly Father

Renew, refresh and regenerate the love of learning in this university.

May research into truth flourish here.

Inspire hearts and minds to thirst after knowledge and to use wisdom in its application.

Let debate illuminate, not obfuscate.

May justice underpin scholarship.

We ask this *in Jesus' name*

Amen

Heavenly Father

We pray that this place of scholarship and academic endeavour may continue to challenge and surprise us, just as your Son still does.

May friendships survive argument and debate.

Bring rigour and humour to life at our university, but let us also draw from the well of divine spirituality that you have provided for us, extravagant God.

We ask this *in Jesus' name*

Amen

Almighty God

Make this university a place where truth is pursued
and you are found.

May minds be stretched and knowledge extended.

Help us to know ourselves better as we debate and write,
test and experiment.

May tutors and those they teach never cease to surprise
and be surprised.

And never let us forget that we are stewards of a world
that you have created.

We ask this *through Jesus Christ, our Lord*

Amen

12

THE LORD'S PRAYER

THE GRACE

THE LORD'S PRAYER

Our Father in heaven,
hallowed be your name,
your kingdom come,
your will be done, on earth as in heaven.
Give us today our daily bread.
Forgive us our sins as we forgive those who sin against us.
Lead us not into temptation but deliver us from evil.
For the kingdom, the power, and the glory are yours,
now and for ever.
Amen

• • •

Our Father, who art in heaven,
hallowed be thy name;
thy kingdom come;
thy will be done;
on earth as it is in heaven.
Give us this day our daily bread.
And forgive us our trespasses, as we forgive those
who trespass against us.
And lead us not into temptation, but deliver us from evil.
For thine is the kingdom, the power and the glory,
for ever and ever.
Amen

THE GRACE

The grace of our Lord Jesus Christ,
and the love of God,
and the fellowship of the Holy Spirit,
be with us all evermore.
Amen

The grace of our Lord Jesus Christ,
and the love of God,
and the fellowship of the Holy Ghost,
be with us all evermore.
Amen

13

THE CHURCH YEAR

PRAYERS FOR SCHOOL ASSEMBLIES AND ALL-AGE WORSHIP

ADVENT

Almighty God

As we begin to prepare for the wonder and mystery of Christmas, we remember the special role of Mary, the mother of Jesus.

You showed her the way through the Angel Gabriel and she responded obediently and joyfully.

Help us to be obedient and joyful in our preparation for Christmas.

Let darkness turn to light as we share the expectation of the season ahead.

We ask this *through Jesus Christ, our Lord*

Amen

• • •

Almighty God

We thank you for the special people who helped to prepare the way for Christmas.

For Moses and the patriarchs of ancient Israel; for the prophets who foretold the news of Christ's coming; for John the Baptist, who paved the way for Jesus; and for Mary who accepted your call to bring your Son into the world.

Come, Lord Jesus, for we await the arrival of the Light of the World.

We ask this *through Jesus Christ, our Lord*

Amen

CHRISTMAS

Heavenly Father

We thank you for all the wonderful things that happen at Christmas; the gifts that we give each other, the love that is shown for those in need.

But, above all, Lord, as the star shone out above Bethlehem on that first Christmas, we thank you for the gift of your Son, the Light of the World.

As Christmas comes, let us join with people down the ages who have celebrated this event and rejoice.

We thank you, Lord

Amen

• • •

Heavenly Father

Make this Christmas special for all here today.

Even if we are unable to give presents, help us to give greetings; even if we do not receive what we want, help us to let people know that we are grateful that they thought of us.

Help us to remember what it was like in that stable in Bethlehem, where the baby Jesus spent his first days with Mary, Joseph and the animals gathered round, shepherds assembled outside and the bright star showing the way to this place, your Son's first home.

We ask this *in Jesus' name*

Amen

EPIPHANY

Almighty God

As wise men came travelling, we pray for travellers at this time of year, joining or leaving family and friends.

Help us to follow the wise men's example to make special efforts to reach out to things that are important, to go the extra mile to do the right thing.

Let us share the special times of Epiphany by honouring the presence of your Son in our lives, just as the wise men honoured the arrival of Jesus in their world so many years ago.

We ask this *through Jesus Christ, our Lord*

Amen

• • •

Almighty God

Just as the star brought the Magi to Bethlehem, create in us the desire

- to travel far to find the truth
- to bring gifts without expecting any in return
- to be open to wonder at your marvellous creation
- to hold on to the power of the Christian story in our daily lives.

Bring us, Lord, closer to you, as your Son's birth brought the wise men to Bethlehem.

We ask this *through Jesus Christ, our Lord*

Amen

HOLY WEEK AND EASTER

Heavenly Father

During this Holy Week, when so much is lost and so much is gained, we remember Jesus' entry into Jerusalem, his betrayal, his suffering, and his crucifixion.

We think of the disciple who claimed not to know him,
the mother who went to the foot of the cross with him
and the Roman centurion who knew this was the Son of God.

Help us to think every day of this week about the feelings of Jesus and all those around him.

We ask this *in Jesus' name*

Amen

• • •

Heavenly Father

At Easter time we pray for new life to come out of the suffering of Jesus on the cross.

We share the joy of the resurrection on Easter Sunday,
just as we shared the sorrow and suffering of Holy Week.

Give us the hope to look forward knowing that our sins have been forgiven.

Help us to understand that out of the agony of Good Friday has come the joy of Easter.

Alleluia, Christ is risen!

Amen

PENTECOST

Almighty God

Bring your Holy Spirit to work in our hearts.

Let the wind and the flames that the disciples felt renew our faith.

Help us to show the Holy Spirit in our lives that others may know your love and learn your way.

We ask this *through Jesus Christ, our Lord*

Amen

• • •

Almighty God

As we celebrate the receiving of the Holy Spirit by the disciples, we ask that we can know the Holy Spirit too.

If we cannot feel this wind in the same way as the disciples, bring us the fruits of the Spirit in other ways.

If we cannot understand or communicate in many tongues,
help us to try to communicate God's love
in the best way we can.

May Pentecost show, in our lives, that we depend on Jesus even though we do not see him, and feel his presence with the help of the comforter, the Holy Spirit.

We ask this *through Jesus Christ, our Lord*

Amen

HARVEST

Heavenly Father

As the harvest is gathered in we praise you for all that is growing and picked and eaten at this time of year.

In thanking you, we also remember the hard work of the farmers who planted and fed and tended the crops, transported the food and made it all available to us.

We take this opportunity also, Lord, to pray for areas of the country and the wider world where crops have failed this year and where food is short.

May communities with plenty help those who have little.

We ask this *in Jesus' name*

Amen

• • •

God of plenty

We thank you for the fruits of the earth at this harvest time.

May we always remember the link between the food on our plate and the fields and farms around us.

Help us to choose and use our food wisely.

Bring food and water to the people who need them and restraint and generosity to the people who have more than enough.

We ask this *in Jesus' name*

Amen

ALL SAINTS' DAY (1 November)

Almighty God

Today we remember all the saints who have shaped the Christian story.

Those who died for their faith, remembering especially . . . . ; those who through their lives and works ensured the foundation of our faith, remembering in particular Mary the mother of Jesus; and those from our own communities and families who have made a difference as Christian people.

We thank you for all those saints who are now at peace with you.

Amen

• • •

Almighty God

You know that we each have our special saints whose lives and works mean a lot to us.

In a moment of silence we remember them now.

Thank you, Lord, for who they were, what they did and what they still mean to us today.

Amen

ALL SOULS' DAY (2 November)

Heavenly Father

On the day of All Souls we remember those who have died, and especially those who are known to us and our families and who are now at peace with you.

Create in us not the fear of death, but grateful thanks for their lives.

Keep away the doubts and dangers of those who are disrespectful of the dead.

Show your love to those who have recently lost someone close to them.

We ask this *in Jesus' name*

Amen

• • •

Heavenly Father

Help us to remember and celebrate the lives of those who have died.

You have shown us through your Son's death and resurrection at Easter that death is not the end, but a new beginning.

In this world, let us not forget all who went before us,
the famous and the little known,
those who died young and those who lived long.

We know you loved them all, Lord, and still love them now.

May we remember and give thanks, may we never forget.

We ask this *in Jesus' name*

Amen

14

PERSONAL 'ARROW' PRAYERS

PERSONAL 'ARROW' PRAYERS

God help me
God lead me
God show me

• • •

Today's a big day for me
Make it a big day for you too, Lord

• • •

Let nothing be in moderation
when we worship you

• • •

Even the ordinary is extraordinary
So let me do the small things well

• • •

Empower me to do your will
Equip me to do it well

• • •

Help me to get the balance right
between family, work and you, Lord

I am yours, Lord
Show me you are mine

• • •

Be close, be near, take away my fear

• • •

Give me the energy to prepare
and the preparedness to surprise

• • •

O God, help me face my class
Bring out the best in me and in my students

• • •

Raise my sights to your horizons, Lord

• • •

Jesus, be my teacher
Jesus, be my friend

• • •

Give me the power to be creative in these moments of peace

Be with me as I am put to the test
Help me to remember how your Son was tested for me

• • •

Help me to be more patient with others and less impatient with myself

• • •

Lord, help me and hold me;
love me and never leave me

• • •

Lord, help me to take responsibility when I need to
and to let go when you say so

• • •

Bring me patience and peace when I really want to let fly

• • •

It's awfully difficult just now, Lord
Calm me with your presence, fill me with your wisdom

• • •

Help me to hear in the noise and listen in the silence

Help me today, Lord, to listen and to learn, and to do all you would want of me

• • •

Grant me peace and integrity when the pressure is on and the going gets tough

• • •

Give me the perseverance to see this task through to the end.

Thank you, Lord